T0039201

Orange
Madrigals

Orange Madrigals

A COLLECTION OF POEMS BY

Arun & Sunitha

PARTRIDGE
A Penguin Random House Company

Copyright © 2015 by Arun & Sunitha.

ISBN: Softcover   978-1-4828-5013-0
            eBook   978-1-4828-5012-3

All rights reserved. No part of this book may be used or reproduced by any means, graphic, electronic, or mechanical, including photocopying, recording, taping or by any information storage retrieval system without the written permission of the publisher except in the case of brief quotations embodied in critical articles and reviews.

Because of the dynamic nature of the Internet, any web addresses or links contained in this book may have changed since publication and may no longer be valid. The views expressed in this work are solely those of the author and do not necessarily reflect the views of the publisher, and the publisher hereby disclaims any responsibility for them.

Print information available on the last page.

To order additional copies of this book, contact
Partridge India
000 800 10062 62
orders.india@partridgepublishing.com

www.partridgepublishing.com/india

But,
if a miracle makes it so
that they're the same as yours...

Contents

Preface

Orange Madrigals is a collection of hundred co-authored poems. The book brings together a set that contributed to a correspondence between its authors – a correspondence that resulted in creating a soulful persona which is at once their lived life and something absolutely not. The poems form an intimate exchange sometimes; sometimes melt into androgynous monologues, or recreate moments from individual memories and dreams closely considered by the other. They fall alternately like exchanges of a mind with the world through the filter of another mind or as exchanges of a mind to the other impeded by the world.

Poetry in our times is understood as a subjective project, very personal. Ever since the canon of Romanticism, the typical poet persona is a mystified individualist. His attitudes, stances, communion with history, and his mythology of the self spontaneously burgeon forth as poems in the troubled, often ostracized or poetic conscience. As for women, creative expressions have been boxed into verbalizations of freedom of sexual choice, and declamations against the abstract of patriarchy, under the historic label 'women's writing'. As these equations run their course into the second decade of the twenty first century, they have brought poetry to a tedious fate, distancing readers, and unintentionally making the art a sort of autoerotic indulgence. *Orange Madrigals* is a collaborative effort whose duplexistential authorship pitches its interests beyond self-examination – it is rather about self-extension, relating and relaying one's self to another of similar mental life, a eugenics of poetry. Poetry as practiced in this book seeks to build a resistance to the usual shelves of poetry that we feed ourselves upon: its dissolution of author-as-a-solipsist addresses squarely the prevalent personae of poets. It hopes to establish how an individual heart need not be the provenance of poetic thought; how it is very possible for two individuals who can communicate, to communicate poetry so as to make it richer, more meaningful, more worth the while an indulgence.

The collection emerges from how we have read life and books, paralleling each other. There is a blurring of ego and personal boundaries where these poems begin. And, as they gather strength and form, the figure of 'poet' as such undergoes a transmutation – two thought-lines merge to create a single poetic comprehension. This comprehension is also informed by the shared attitudes towards literature and philosophy, and the tryst with contemporary Indian and world poetry. Actually *Orange Madrigals* is not a book that was planned as such. The authors had written verse and prose together for the last six years before assembling poems for the book. It started as mutual reading and editing of drafts of poetry, but soon became a give and take of poetic raw materials ranging from dreams and subjective pasts to formats and vocabulary.

It was common in the older days to create poetic worlds through creating poetic selves that had little or nothing to do with confessing autobiographical truths. Poetry was a fantastic function then, a metamorphosis of the everyday, a mass that one could approach only with a sense of mystery. As it evolved to modern contexts, identity politics and political persuasions became an overbearing preoccupation to poetic writing, especially in postcolonial poetry. Poems, for the large part, adapted to the environment and became platforms to state the necessities of ethnicity, gender or *realpolitik*. Though this collection does not take after any great tradition consciously, or furnish nostalgias for any older poetry, including the by-now rooted Indian English poetic canon, it is such that we bear in mind the 'sense of artistic purpose' of older works. Usually, poems are better engaged if one understands their purposes, methods, backgrounds to their content, and the secrets behind the authorial will to create.

The collection experiments with various types of structures and formats of poetry, including sonnets, free verses, prose poems and slam poems; our materials also vary widely, from traffic junctions to spiritual transcendence. The poems have been exchanged between each other freely. Sometimes lines were borrowed, and sometimes interpretations of experiences. Sometimes poems formed of themselves independently, as if they were of a third voice manifesting with a will of one's own. They use male and female experiences of the world and the word freely without concentrating on confessional honesties. The book by genesis is dialogical, its conception of authorship and subjectivity open. Every poem is lit by bright conversations between the authors, a giving, a free flight of two intelligences before an utterance. The book as a whole submerges *personal* expression. Co-authorship is a transgressive play of personalities, one author emboldened by the protective cover of the partner. Sometimes we have struggled to perceive

the identity (ies) and voice (s) of our poems. That is
what is most spectacular about co-authoring, creating
a third person, a third voice that rises on its own,
confusing the authors even for themselves. Therefore
the best in this set belongs simultaneously to both
and neither of us. The book is monovocal: we have
removed the origins of individual words, sections, and
lines, although they contain traces of the collaborative
process – these poems could pass as the creation of a
solo consciousness, but they become still richer if read
as collaborations. The blending of language or refusal
of authorial boundaries contributes to the vagaries of
our poetry. Co-authoring is an ethic and aesthetic here
a testing of rules, conventions and prejudices.

If the poetry here can be construed as a story –
and there is a fair chance this thought may appear to
you as you start seeking out characters, events and
morals – its plot would be somewhat as follows: an
existential drama of an androgynous persona in its
own highly specific coloration and character. The story
begins morning and journeys through a flux of past and
present and ends in a distant night when it rains. In
between, the narrator's soul spans its impressions, its
past, its disappointments, its expressions and failures
at expressions, its jubilations, frustrations, desires,
and vacuums. For this 'story' is titled as a version of
lyric, madrigals, it may be regarded as an elaborate
pronouncement of an inner music too. This music was
imagined to be orange in colour: bright and round,
fragrant and pert like oranges just picked – one could
peel it and savor its secret tangy sweetness. This
music was imagined to be orange in colour: like the
sun that floats above the water it emerged from, or is

about to immerse into – a riotously silent orange. From mushy little pronouncements to long lean meditations, the range of this orange music also constitutes an unmasking of the relation between its authors, a demystification of it, and sometimes a parody of an erotic-religious myth. In other words, an angle to the totality of our emotional universe is presented here: garnered, with its musical, metrical instances; humor and irony; and even the dryly prosaic, diaristic moments.

Listening close to these poems, what could a reader hear? Let us offer a wishful response: first, a taut music – sung together at times, at others taking turns. Instead of rotund mellifluousness you would encounter abrupt strings, lasting in general, only short whiles. You would listen to a vocabulary which, in its search for expressive efficacy, stretches from archaic English to local transliterational variations. The reader may find thematic reiterations in the body of *Madrigals,* at times, to the point of obsession. And at times, these lyrics are curt and compressive guards at the gates of unwelcome spaces of mental meanderings. We have known how words-as-poems take the reader away from his comfort zone of meaning-making, but have also seen the way meaning-making creates alternate universes of harmony for him. In sum, we believe, our readers would co-experience our will to refocus, to renew the time-honored materials of poetry by submitting them to fresh challenges.

We have here, as they were called at different times in different places, hundred bottled messages, hundred well-wrought urns, hundred capsules of punishable secrets, hundred verbal icons, a hundred

pseudo-persons. Our attempt through them was to
make sense of the chaos – both personal and cultural –
and in this, to achieve forms of expressions that will
suit intentions. What is clear in *Orange Madrigals*,
besides the personal intensity and creative will, is the
impact of multiple forces through which we rose to this
utterance. Cities, journeys, passions, defeated loyalties,
slippages, platonic shifts between generations – all
these have informed the poetry we have attempted to
collect. *Orange Madrigals* is the beginning of a quest
for valid terms to express our relationship with life, at
large.

Arun
&
Sunitha

1. Dawn

Time skins another night:
Sacral blood leaps
Scarlet in clouds.

A quiver -
Twigs night had tacked together
Unstick and lash back.
The drenched grass
Exhales steamy mist.

A Birth.
Time bows Eastwards.

2. Outside Inside

Flowing in through the window
Stretched from the green beautiful
A stream yellow bright

A golden strip
From the blue unknown
Into the room

Shining and fading
A sunny warmth of happiness

A mirror on the floor
Shining double
Numerous
As I walk into it
A countryside within my room

3. Waking

You draw back your eye-lids
And relent two dream-anointed beams of brightness.

Two windows open
In the distance
To usher the sparkles
Suffused in the mist:
Sleep uncoils and slides off from the chairs,
Night stretches and jumps tail on end, off the tables
And the corner quickens to a warm waiting.

4. This Road to You

This road to you
Doesn't stop at you
But crosses you
In a swift adieu
And flies to the cobalt blue
Lines of hills that issue
A river that floods
With words and glows
In balmy silences –

We set out again, the two, on this road that made
us one;
This road, so much like love: unexpected curves
Ever breaking into unaddressed landscapes.

Strands kissing,
Sticking, ticking
And tickling
Piercing, at times
The eye
At others
Trespasses to the mouth
Flirting with
The wind,
Playful,
Flying loose
From grips
And high
And coquettish
And unruly
Tremulous and
Dancing.
The wind ceases:
The dance fizzles.

6. As Good as the Other

Strangers knocked at your door:
You kept it bolted shut
And through the window
Gave them winters
Till their souls became
Hoarse hyena howls.

Strangers came to my door:
I gave them the keys
To my library, wardrobe, and cellars
And left the house.

Only: my homelessness
Was safe behind your doors.

7. The Peanut Vendor

Tintin tintin tin
Here comes the peanutman
Yellow green and orange in brine
As the sun in the horizon shines.

Pushing and shoving his trolley forward
Salty water lashing onward
Shouting of peanuts amla and lime,
Mangoes and carrots and slices of pineapples.

Tiny trots in fun and frolic
Grabbing glassy ice-sticks
Marbles green and wheels yellow on palms little
Smacking and winking as tongues tittle.

Lollipops and lozenges sweet
Salted peanuts pendulous on heat
Pellets in cones cozy and warm
Fingers dig in, and put them to calm.

Tin Tin tintintin
Here comes the peanutman
Yellow green and orange in brine
As the sun in the horizon shines.

8. The Jungle

Cars creeping and swishing.
Animals numerous:
Hippos, dinosaurs and beetles.
Buses, giant caterpillars
Vrooming past
Autolungs on the move
Puffing and choking.
Bikes, black ants
Exploding acid bombs
Bagging ignition packs
Mirror ears
Each to its own
Yet a part of the other
In line
Stopping and moving
Chasing the one
Before being chased by the one behind
Pushing and shoving
Screeching and punching
Denting and shattering
And lying in puddles
Of red,
The line broken, moves
Again,
Into another
And leaves
The other behind to
Follow, overtake and shift

From one to the other
Automated
Tremulous
Changing
Never ending.

9. The Mask

It bothered me to wear the author's mask that was
hanging on this wall. A mask always needs to have a
face inside, to become a mask. So in a way, without
this botheration on my part, the mask would not ever
function. I pushed my face in the mould and felt the
welcoming vacuum: I shall belong to it.

After fixing the mask, I held my breath. A trembling
noise crawled on my face.
I sensed vaguely that the mask was digging a hole
in my consciousness – a hole that eats up along
with chunks of memories, unexpected fringes of
conversations and contours of unforgettable sights.
I was warned in a dream later, of storms forming at
the horizon.

10. Twilight

I said you are growing old
He said so are you my child

I said you are weak
He said you are my strength

I said you do not know, the times have changed
He said, I have not

I said they will hurt you, tear you
He said I am in tatters

I asked, why don't you learn
He smiled

I said yours is a wasted life
He was silent

I looked into his eyes of pain
My fingers slowly searching for his
Met their trembling companion

A lightning split my heart
I the daughter
He the father

11. My Name

I hear you call it again.
I have lent it to some before,
Kept it from some,
And though rarely,
Even changed it for some.

I had put it letter by letter in boxes,
And made totems out of it.
But after the excursions
It always came back like
A sullen and silent child.

A history more proper than its bearers',
An essence deeper than a lifetime of wear:
A name always keeps to itself half its secret.

Time in spate froths off its silt on a name –
A fine silt that glistens in the Sun,
Throbs in rain, hardens in winter.

You weeded it
And sowed a dandelion;
See, it has sprung again –
Each silvery down in its fluff
Alert, glowing, as you call it.

I hear you.

12. The Heart that Beats Out There

The heart that beats out there is not yours,
The blood nothing like the warm pools of past
Shooting through your nerves,
Its mired throb not yours,
Nor its pangs.

But,
if a miracle makes it so
that they're the same as yours

You step beyond the facade of the present,
Shed mantles of proud solitude,
Burn the coloured effigies that command you

And open arms
To quench with sun a sea that wakes in you.

13. Dear Window

Dear window
You are an animal
We caught and framed,
And taught: Silence, Patience, Reflection.

Do not forget
It is through your soul
That our days,
Like slow mountaineers
Breath, shudder and
Vanish to invisible heights.

Dear window
You are that animal
Whose deep eyes we shall not rub close
Once we collect our rewards and retire.

Do not forget:
You are the animal
That accompanies us to the Beyond
As we climb the vertiginous snow,

As everything else falls with muffled cries
Into a whiteness,
Behind us.

14. Train Number 7229 from Hyderabad to Trivendrum Central Crosses the Kerala Border

Train number 7229 scuffs and paces the sun-scattering silvery rails of bare and remote villages. Mud-walled houses, like startled raccoons, rise, stare and turn away as soon.

Railway-gates where vehicles wait and watch.

Windswept platforms throwing up desolate benches.

Huge haphazardly lying boulders basking naked in the plateau sun.

I sit back as the light fails outside: into eyes that aren't looking at anything come a hand that swings a lantern, a pattern of lights left behind in a town, a cold bulb lighting an empty street circle, a shadowy mansion with one of its top-storey rooms still lit – someone reading?

Train number 7229 races into the wet morning with its one and twenty sooty coaches, thumping through more bare and bushy villages. Sunlight slowly filling the panes, tall green trees swinging their smiles, a river shying away amongst glistening sand – the train leaps and catches up the seven minutes it was late for Kanjikkod.

15. Summer Rain: at 3 p.m.

A scorching afternoon turns
to cool darkness and
the rain shells
water-pebbles on you;
drops and beads drench you;
the smell of softening earth and slopping water.

Free from sweat and
Sweat slaked clothes and
Smells of sheets, pillows and beds that
Like sponges sucked sweat.

Unlike the salty sundrops that leave a stain
Are these beady notes
That play on you
And roll down
Into nothingness.

16. The Appointment

A smile died on her dusky face
As her bird picked my tarot-card.
She twitched in her sharaai, said:

"Watch the faithless word –
breaking the watch and ward –
catching you all off guard:
you strike, grovel, demur,
but still it nails you down
with all those vacuous vows,
debts deferred, pledge forgone
to end it once for all".

A smouldering new nakedness
Devoured the old magical clothes;
I hobbled back from oracles
And laid me in a mummy-case.

The dusk that ominously hung
Outside the sinister windows
Bled one drop scarlet poison
Into the violet horizon.

A ballerina on snow
Gliding and sliding eyesome
Smoothly with grace
Clad in black lace
Leaving tracks that move
Parallel, cuts and swerves
Blade-linings on ice:
The ballet allays
A balletomane, your eyes.

18. Pebbles

They kept falling –
Pebbles - in the lake –
Making circles smooth-expanding
Around gulping dips,
Lapping each other's make.

As they cease
The sounds retreat.
In silence, the lake is an expanse
Of flickering sense
From a ceremony just recessed.

The pebbles rest
Sunk fathoms deep
Shaking loose musty bottom-dust.
They'll soon cool and
Gather a full and sated chest:

Those stones that scraped the sun-baked banks.

19. A History of Poets

We Poets sift the harvest of speech
In a filter-net swung from one to the other
Beside the fields of History
Like we always knew this,
And always this well.

Age by sieving age, chaff accrues;
The cherished little grain gets
Carefully stored away
In millions of throbbing pink chambers
Across the neverending map
Along the neverceasing clock.

Some of us leave sons,
Some leave memorials,
And some, searing sighs.

But, there is this simple bird out there
That visits these granaries
In unseen hours
By the lunette-windows
And pilfers from the store
With a mystic lift

Silently spelling its swift flight
In and out.
The grace of her transparent sky
Transforms of our store
To an eternal lore.

20. Devolving

Bones stick out
As I feel you,
Your aged shoulders
Cranked with life –
A shredded self
Spread in Time –

21. After a Rainy Night

It rained torrents last night
And as usual the power failed:
Sitting in the dark, I listened
To the mayhem outside.
The wind turned and returned to the windows
As if emitted from the howling nostrils of
An angry elemental god.

In the morning, when I opened the window
The trees were still, scared, and bent
Amid a sprawling calm that spread around them,
And the fused-out bulb in the verandah hung
Like a heavy drop of water
That froze forever in smoky fear.

22. Loving on a Sunday Afternoon that Flowed in Through a Clear Glass-Window

Bright gold of the ripe day oozes over
The succumbing petals of the bedside flowers;
Your goldfish breathes, wide-eyeing us from its clear
bowl.

All noon we lay naked on the bed
Not once looking at the bodies
That had by now returned to their own skins.

The afternoon held time in a limbo
And we slept and woke,
Breathing the slow heat,
Breaking golden sweat,

Until the ring in your sleepy hand
tugged at my hair and broke the illicit spell.

23. Non sequiturs

A heart asked

Why so much of love

A heart replied

How do I love you more

24. And My Hand Slips from Yours

I feel myself moving
Away
Away from you and them
I try to hold myself here
But the tears that well in you
The pain I see in your eyes
Tears me apart
Further and further
Away from you and myself.

The tired scraping legs that
You drag along
The slow loud breath that keeps you alive
Takes me off
Into a far and lonely hive
Of pain and silence heavy:
I stretch my hands to you,
Unnoticing, you move past
Past me
Talking to others in a voice
Weak and strained
A voice beaten –
A life defeated –
Into old age and neglect
And solitude;
Your world shred
By your own.

I, left helpless, a watcher,
My hands hearkening to help
But hanging in midair,
I, with a heart
Heavier and by moments heavier
Till thoughts of death loom:
Of yours... mine...mine own,
Till death eats inside me and
Leaves me a nothing.

A spell that leaves me dazed
Dazed in fear
A fear of death
That chokes me with its dead life.

And again I look up
And see, only your face,
Its impending loss,
Your fear of death,
Of leaving me behind,
Alone:

And my hand slips from yours.

25. Controls

Harangues: no more words
Only exhausted tirades
That fail to notice absences,
Tireless talkers half blind, full deaf.

Virtually dismissed by
The buoyant young
Until the breath fails
On these ageing specimens
Moaning and contorted
Dribbling from the mouth

I slide and keep gliding
Through the crowd
My feet on fire
Unable to stand still
No water could quench
Nor calm the scalding heat
Groping my way along
The unknown paths before
Waiting to stumble on a wall
And stop dead and calm
Things escape: they are
No longer in control of me.

26. A Gradient Noon

A gradient noon -
Dark and wan -
A blanket of drops
Scouring dusty leaves
Into green and yellowgreen -
A soaring auburn dryness.
Heaving up the nostril, the wet earth.
Crumpled and defeated,
Carried hither
Thither
An unknown memory
Sails over the gushing raindrops
And drowns in vigour.

And is washed away beyond sight, to drain when the
drops cease.

27. At the End of the Day

At the end of the day
Am I to leave you,
A step before the other
Taking me farther
And farther
Into the distant vast
And you in a corner
Vacant
Reeled to me as I to you
Gazing at the creeping void
Sharing a heart heavy
Words unsaid
Minds conversing
A quiet unease
Searching
To comprehend
The largeness of
A presence
As thoughts and beaded notes.

28. Careless Wishes

I wish I was a baby boy sleeping,
my feet hanging loose and naked
from the tired seat of a lunging bus
while the sun is going down outside,
with your arms around me,
with your dreams filling my head.

I wish the world would show
the least care for us
as a supple wind blows us:
blows us both to a long long night.

29. Narcissus

The mirror opened:
a small creek.
It let out a sparrow
that hung on the frame
and looked at me –
O, those beady eyes!

A cool wind noses into the glass-doors.

I rest my head on the mirror-pane.

The shades grew long in the yard outside,
and the fat leaves of those unknown trees broke
sweat.

I could be buried here.

30. Exile

The dust swept over the harvested field putting it to a
dull sleep
And withdrew with the wind into a scraggly bush.

I was very happy as a child –
Far away from this baking Sun.
In the evenings, I used to swing on the hanging
banyan roots
Till dusk perched coolly on my shoulders.

Anesthetic coolness
of the plateau-evening.

I remember how in the evenings
We wore the rain all the way home from school,
Mouth and eyes gaping open, running against the
striking rainthreads,
My vision always smarted till late night in
monsoons.

The dead-snake road winds ahead,
Beyond the sparsely leaved trees.

It felt good to fall in love back at my place.
I remember how she fluttered and then shut her eyes
as our faces started to blur in an intense proximity.

It's dusk in the head.
I listen to the dizzy procession of waves
In a sea that I haven't seen now for years.

I wasn't looking till the rain smuggled back in its entirety
All the ghosts to my hostel walls, in spreading water-blotches.

I sleep with naked nightmares
Breeding in miraculous fuss
Maggot-like memories
That crawl up to my windows,
Tap, sigh and wait for a reply.

I am tired.
Oh, to think
The silliest illusion
Is the hardest to lose.

31. Borrowing

I borrow your sorrow to comprehend this dusk
That like a bonfire soars and embodies
Questions I carry about us.

I borrow your words to write poetry
That like a rain thrilling the sea vanquishes
Questions I carry about us.

32. Thanatos

Years later
miles away
my back no more holds me straight
and the lifelines
inch from my palm
to travel up your opening hands.

33. Remainder

Life, like doors straining on hinges
Breath, like moaning wind
Plump drops like stray pebbles in shallow wells,
Air, sweet rising,
Water accumulated, puddles -
The remainder of a deluge
now spent.

34. A Bizarre Bed-time Rhyme

There were chess-pieces three:
Two of them were queens,
The third one but a pawn.

The queens had all the moves,
Panache and good élan;
They fought till ghastly sea

Turned blood in every wee.
Odalisques of their clans
Cheered them on and on.

The king mighty observes
From his chequered throne:
What mire! What pity!

The war worsened: every
Sword in clam'ring tones,
The moors imbued sanguine.

And lo, suddenly queens
Both fall mutually slain.
The noises cease quickly

As someone shuts the board.
The war was done, mated.
The game long since ended.

Surprised, a life began:
The king had become pawn;
The pawn, a headstrong queen.

35. The Cozy Sleep

Flapping sheets flat
Bulging pillow big
Flicking
Frolicking
In the fan's whirring wind,
Tickled and heaved up
The cozy sleeper
Sleeps.

36. A Vineyard Within

Your name ripens variedly
On the myriad vines of my soul
And every soft wind
Fells a bunch
And fills my moments;
And like full purple grapes
Crushed in winepresses
Burst into a primal sweetness.
Frothing, the must readies,
A strong heady red oozes
Over a beady-bubbled dawn
Onto a world called us.

37. Commuter 2

Whizzing past at
Breakneck speed
Across the winding
Maze-like space,
Hairbreadthscape,
Gasps,
Frenzied eyes,
Hanging jaw,
The meditative commuter commutes
Invitations of
A paid suicide.
Thought-stuck,
Letting trees, fields, birded skies, rivers swish past.
As the journey ends
Not packed, or laid out,
But still, and silent
And
Ready for another
And another and
Another...

38. Morning Rain

A morning rain sweeps up the night's silence;
Wet winds blow her name on my skin,
And shock its memory.
Like a coop of invisible chicks
Rain goes about its cackling search
Around the house.

My longing is like
The dawns of Scheherazade:
Pulsing incomplete stories
That buy dear days off death's store.

Amid the far-strewn mist and dampness
I sense her warm body leaving the city, for me:
Soaring through drenched traffic junctions,
Off above bridges and shivering rivers,
Past flooded lanes,
A mother heavy with milk,
A beloved light with pleasure,
A sister carrying ripe oranges
Tucked away in her skirt –
A warmth leaving the city,
For me.

39. Bubbles

I took my new poem to her,
A good poem it was.
She read it
And we discussed how
It falls in place with the new cryptic genre:
We saw that the images held together well.
One of us, must be me, even gave count of the
syllables
To say how much of a haiku the poem was.

Later I remembered that she never asked who the
poet was:
Something within me burst like a soap-bubble in
the sun.

40. Rhyme for a Morn

Eyelids heavy with sleep
Thoughts stretching to peep
Dreams unspoken
Spill into the open

Soon put to sleep
Eyes sluggish, hung and deep
Kiss the other in a leap

Flashes flickering off and on
A heaviness spreading this dawn
That blinks and blushes into a morn

41. (Breaking) Silence

Silence is a rock mussel:
fibrous clots clamp
the rough mouth, wide.
The pell-mell life, within the vise,
delicately crawls its porcelain smooth habitat,
and tempts
a flashing knife to swim the fatal mile.

42. Land-stork

The unwinking eye-button of the land-stork;
The beak's polished ochre
Combs the yellowed grass for prey:
The moment does not have meanings –
The moment is the meaning.

A shock of its neck to the ground –
An eyeful of white whooping wings –
A spasm of the wind –
Is the only memory of violence.

The rest, like before, is a zen koan.
The bird slowly wade the sky cloud by floating cloud.

43. Just to Record that I Remembered Us

I set on this whiteness
Two coffee-brown marbles (that turn mud-red
when wet);
Two honeyed black currants (alert, pert – throbbing
to touch);
A glistening black tuft (or a bird's silky perch);
Two dark-skinned moments (with love teeming in
between).

Just to record I remembered us
I set on this whiteness
A whiter expanse (of two souls in free flight).

44. Spell

A spell is cast:
Rolling out in
Beautiful calligraphy.
Out of the quill
Onto the blank
Rolled out, smoothened.
Fingers yield to the spell
Twisting and turning,
Oblique and lean.
As clouds of thoughts
Stretch and straighten
Out in the open
And are glued and pinned
To the white
Unleash,
And lose themselves:
The ever-radiant and new
Wait yet,
To be moulded and
To yield
To the magic wand.

45. Poems from the Capital

1. Night Train

They squeeze out of the snake's sides
And break like poison in blood
Into the shimmering black night.

A grey heart
Bursts on the streets:
I drink my mouthful of silence.

A fig tree washes its
Hair in the sea:
I clothe my shame with a lie.

The moon ploughs up a furrow
And sows gathered tears:
I broke a star from the sky.

Dragging its glimmering body
The train raced up the snaky railroad
Deep in the shimmering night.

2. Seeds

Seeds stirred
beneath the wet asphalt
as rain wept out
her forest hours
again, this year.

Again, this year
as rain confessed
her desert hours
seeds basked
in the shining confession.

Rain broke
into crystals
on dripping black branches
of oblivious trees.

Rain spun
a glassy mausoleum
round the black branches
of senile trees.

Rain broke
at the sheen
of the soaked earth.

The shining fragrance
of the wet earth
broke her desert fears.

Seeds stirred.

3. Savior Angel

It is a holy augury
That you solemn guard:

Night breaks an icy rosary –
Beads thaw in the yard –
I almost sense your shimmery
Fingers in my heart
Nuzzling dreamy gossamery
Silhouettes – they chart
To gold and warmth that unbury
The Sun – the Eye – the Word.

4. Metaphors that Survived the Last Blast

It's not about the dirt.
It's not about reducing
One to a faith or to a flag
As they talk about it later from radiant relay rooms.
It's about the skyfall
Over your mindscape
After the crescendoing beeps.

It's the steel that gradually settles in one's eyes;
the slow loss of lilies in the touch;
the way words lean to rub rough pubic thatches.
It's the lies that branch and grow leaves
and burst into fragrant shocks of unfamiliar flowers.

Its about how the innocent feet on the sands fail their
grace.

It's about silence chronically sleepwalking to a region
of animal racket;
the milk of solitary meditations churning up tufts of
hair and toxic violet.

It's about the endlessly kindled recurrence of it all
till a fire claims it to stock-still urns
or a rot claims it to wetness.

It's about lights that
darken the way.

46. The Room after You Leave

Can you imagine this place after you leave?
The fans still doing their circles,
Now audibly tired –
The windows dreaming of the blink they earned
Lids apart since morn –
Noises from corridors that settle,
Like dust on leaves, in my ears –
People are characters that lost their stories
Floating like leaves on an evening pond
That shivers in night-ward ripples –
Can you imagine?

I hear them calling my name, but won't budge:
I might lose this dream
That isn't broken
Yet.

47. Profile

Wired to the world I sit.
Weighing a few extra memories,
Watching unnerving shadows,
Interpreting vagaries of flesh, I, sit.

And in luminous pixels, my dreams split.

48. Out of the Sea

The wave of your silence crawls over
And bites
On the candescent sands
And ebbs –
With a half-moon off my heart.

49. Last Rites

Body of the day in cold-storage:
I strewed loosely the ivory grist
Of your Si
len
ce
And
Left the stamen
Of my latest thought
Stuck on the gasping block of ice.

50. Rainbow

He brought a poem to me,
A good poem it was.
I read it
And we discussed how
Its cryptic genre
Held its images together
Like us — a Haiku.

Its words reflected in his eyes,
A rainbow deepened within me,
And I never asked who the poet was.

51. Mirror, Images

I watch her from the bed
As she stands herself
Before the tall wooden-frame mirror
Studying her naked torso:
Thin bowed shoulders
Bracketed drooping breasts.

She moves her hands over her belly
And gathers the folds of skin that hang loose
From her navel to the stubbly pubis.

Desire and humiliation swept over me:
Bodies that chronicle lust and excitation
Wither like books, and grow fond for readers
And silverfish, alike.

52. An Other Story

Tried to love:
Ended in pain.
Each loving his own way
Different from mine.
Unable to comprehend mine,
Knowing it as indifference
Selfishness and irritation.
And I too learned
To live their way:
To them love,
To me else.

53. A Local Fair

There are men and women
Dancing in my head:
Young men with broken feet
Grope their partners with painted nails.
The fair is filling up silently with dust;
The stale air of a decaying town.
You couldn't have passed this place!

I put my hand over my heart.

54. Elements and Us

You are the earth
And I the sky.

You send me your birds
Every once in a while
I give them the clouds
The sun and the wind.

I send you my rains
Every once in a while
You give them the thirst
The song and the Sea.

55. Ocean

And now:
it is easy to forget
what I came for

among so many who have always
lived here

swaying their gilded fans
between the bright blue-green reefs

and,
besides,
down here,

you breathe differently.

I came to explore the wreck.

I came to see the damage that was done
and seek the treasures that prevail.

I came for the wreck
and not the story of the wreck;

for the drowned faces hiding
away from the oozing sun:
the evidence of damage.

This is the place.

And I am here,
And I have company:
the mermaid whose dark hair
blackens the stream.

We shall circle silently
about the wreck,
the bodies and all
and quite unseen,
one dark day,

dive headlong to the trove-hold deep.

56. Silver

A Double before me:
Hands wandering over
My face, my body.
Your eyes,
Staring back at me,
Lips smiling and frowning,
The wonder, the duplexistence – you
of silver
and the silver of you,
An image inside a hard icy river,
Mimicking me, cynically
Pushing and thrusting
Me into your self,
Forcing yourself to thoughts evasive
Pining for a fleshy self
A lost self
Of thoughts that gush into the silver.
Who are you?
I myself, yet different.
Touching you, I feel
Cold ripples that do not accept
My yearning fingers.
To know you
Who stares at me
Not knowing who I am,
Caught in the silvery river
Trying to tell me
Who I am,
Unable to in a

Robotic freeze,
Without an individual life,
Existence as
One yet two
Distant and familiar,

It's not you
It's me... I,
Our gaze into each other,
Into mutual depths
Caught in whirlpools
Of fleeting thoughts,
Into hazy tunnels,
Meeting you time and again
Whenever the silver appears
In the house and on the streets
Lingering or fleetingly swiped
My eyes looking into yours
Fingers softly touching yours
You in the silver
And the silver in you.

57. Forgotten Photographs

Wasting away -
To nothingness -
A life spent on others -
Out of love -
Morphed into memories
Piled
In a life toppled
Unable to gather
The vastness encircling
Into a palmful
Of happiness and youth
Drained -
Long forgotten
Amidst photographs
In the album
Of Life.

58. Words like Birds

Words like birds out of me fly into the open. Only to fly higher and higher. And away from me. I am left alone, standing on this shore watching a part of me fly away, leaving my grasp, never to return. Happily making homes elsewhere. To be lost in eternity. To leave a lone figure groveling in loneliness for more.

I dream I tumble from skyways,
Hang onto a dandelion,
And land safe in a lilting boat
Where talking, sadly, makes no sense.
Confused I dip a fingertip
In the Sunward flowing stream.

And wake up to see
My hands have lost their sense of touch.

60. The Other End of Care

As I tread and place one feet before the other
Leaving behind many
Already walked and shed
A knowledge of moments spent
Leaves me tired and bent.
Beautiful moments, childhood,
Holding hands and being cared,
Of outings together and sharing each, the other.

Unknowingly my hold slips
From the one being held into the one to hold.
The firmness now fragile and weak,
Trembling and stumbling
For being reliant on another.
A heaviness looms
And wrings my heart.

61. Distance

The distance between you and me is unreal:
sometimes it shrinks to a speck and dissolves, but
then, as soon, expands and throws us seas apart.
Worse, once written, this fact becomes either poetry
or raving, and not the felt experience.

When I say I'm not alone anymore, I keep my life
at some distance away from your life – the distance
needed for you to support me. But that distance
between you and me is unreal too. You could be
thrown far apart the next moment – so far apart
where I mightn't even exist for you.

The only real within us is an alternate version of life.
A version that burns down broken promises, rusty
lies and trials and errors of mismatched passions. But
that, when written, becomes either poetry or raving.

62. Lethe

Little drops that sail
Keep sailing
To a place unfamiliar -
Hurrying past me as I sit blinking at them

Eyes tracking and following
From end to endlessness,
Never reaching: chained
to others taking off
to complete the journey.

In haste glassy marbles move
To be sucked into earth somewhere far
and vanish.

For the rain does stop:
the bubbles burst
and scatter
dry drops of oblivion.

63. Motor-maimed

Honking through the roads
The traffic whizzing, scraping and just-not-scraping:
Fastened to your vehicle
Blinking eyes you exist.

Red.
Stop.
Still.
An impatient engine revs
Waiting to take off.

Green
And Vrooooom......
While another stillness revs
And balks at signals.
Crossing
Life and Death.
Yellow orange
And
Red.

Eyes peering and peeping
Into the next
Glancing at signals
Shouting and roaring
The road
The anger
The abuse
The sarcasm –

And the roadrunner takes off
Again
Towards destination
One in a million.

64. A New Year Wish
for the Past Lover

Our memories
All of a sudden
Seemed so beautiful yesterday
When I saw you pass
Under those morning trees
Rustling their morning leaves.

Nothing.

The soft assuring perfume on your skin,
Your sharp coffee brown eyeballs:
Now that we are done with each other,
All that has blurred.

And those memories
Seemed so beautiful
As you passed yesterday
With a peculiar nonchalance
Under those morning leaves,
Drops from your wet untied hair
Sticking satin wrinkles to your back.

Nothing,
I just wanted to say
You did betray
Though you did a great job of hiding it
Your sidelong glances
To where I should have been standing
With a New Year wish.

65. The Cat

The cat is simply everywhere on a given day.
On the culvert sleeping, his ears keeping watch;
In the shade purring angrily at himself clutching the
earth;
Out in the sun as a proud machine-perfect movement
of limbs;
At the wayside trashcan licking wet the dry fish
bones:
Always involved most in himself.

Or he scratches the truck parked by the roadside,
Thumps dying moths with soft white paws,
One moment here and the next, up, on the tree,
Busy at some self-occupied spree,
Till the sun goes down.

Then in dark, he spits out daylight
Through two sulfur balls in his head
And looks at the moon's skeletal white face
To study the scratch patches closely.

66. Rashmi Dances Beautifully, and Works for an M N C

She flicks my eyes
With a mudra
To the left of the stage:

"Look!
The moon has come down
To graze along the hilltop.
Krishna, the Lord, is playing his mesmeric flute
Somewhere In the honey-enwombed sylvan arcades
of Brindaban
And –
"Arre! Look to the right!!"
- Engrossed gopis
Walk out of their homes in half-sleep"

At night
As we shared our dinner
She, but, seemed not so comfortable
Fidgeting in the chair
Giving strained smiles
Eyes not where they were best;
All the way saying something else too
Than what she was saying.
To know that her body could be so sure of
Each tiny muscle-twitch and every single lift or drop
of eyebrows
Only an hour ago!

But I have seen this before:
Her office in her mind,
After performance nights,
She behaves like a wild tree in flower
Somehow fit into a cubicle.

"Well, Rashmi, enough!
The week's work is done.
And you *do* remember, right...?"

"Are, haan, it's New Year yaar..."

> – Her sudden laughter peeled
> like stubborn sunrays
> into the December night.

67. Write 1

Words gush in and flow
And I in pain gush forth as words
Not tears
For words keep back tears
Keep my thoughts
For the drops to come
Even when grown faint
These words of pain
Words for you
Those paired eyes wrinkled and spent
Who have made me flow like this
For you
Forever this heart will pine
And in pining forget to live
For you have made this life
And made me live
In forgetting to live.

Still my pen moves today
Unwilling to stop or pause
As I fill page after page
Of what is in me
Words smoothly flow in agony
Words of a spent life
Words heavy floating around
Words of heat and uneasiness
Words not of music but
Of Life
A life lived in hope
A hope misplaced on others.

Stop I say
Stop STOP
As I always tell myself
Stop or else this madness
Will never end
And in not ending will...
Will bring forth more...
More and more
So Stop.
Words
Leave me to my thoughts.

And words smiled at me
For thoughts are words
Yes, you words are not enough
For these are those you can only grapple with
Words fail
I too will cease one day
Having no more words
And my silence which speaks now
Too will end and fail to speak
As now
Words falter even now
Going from one end to the other
Failing to complete at others
You too falter
Like me
Like them
Like all.

I find myself unable to use you
Then what is this I am doing?
Using you to lay myself on clearness
Moving through into out above below you
Beautifully skidding and sliding from one to the other
As this pen makes me do
Is this how you feel as you fall and adorn paper
Thoughts to words to pen to paper?

How do you feel as you lie black on white
Waiting to be taken and caressed by a hand
Who knows you,
Not to be ruffled and mocked at by rough hands?

I see you smiling as I write this
As you fall in place one after the other smoothly gliding,
Yes, I know you as I pour myself into you
With an ease as never before
I can see you smile knowingly
Of days of darkness you will go through
Before being in the open again
Before eyes that read meaning
And know you
Fondle you into life
As the fingers firmly hold the words leaping onto you
The selfsame fingers that water you
Under whose weight you bow
And nod, left with rolling marbles of green tint
To raise your head in the eve' when the sun drops into
the cold sea
To rise and smile at the calm cool around
The smell of soil as it bathes and wafts around in water
Searching for the shadows before in the sun

All wet in the showers falling
Bent in the sun and now in the eve
Spreading happiness with your
Red pink yellow blue green
Dropping into drowsiness and sleep
As the day winds and the life.

68. Hollowing Out

Boring into the body,
Then to the soul,
My very being –
The borer thick,
Dark and agitated,
Unsure –
Into the head
And into my
Consciousness,
A drone
Drilling past,
Now fast,
Faster and faster
Slowing to a white
Piercing silence.

69. Write 2

The witching hour past, the night grows sane.
The wisps of yellow sun pulseless remain
Enclosed in bluish pods half-poignant:
The dreamless slumber of tired children.

Now, pass the silver knife of poetry,
Write, operate the womb of memory.

70. Black and White

Crispy pristine white
Inviting
To break asunder
Black words like
Scattered sesame
Racing one behind the other
Eyes at heels
Fixed on each
Black
Foregrounded against
The white
A vision of white
Through the black
A transparent black
Imbued with white
Each vacant
Separated from the other
The eyes chasing, capturing
And conquering
The ever yielding black
To the very last white.

71. Whenever She Kisses Me

Whenever she kisses me –
I keep eyes steadfastly shut:

Lest the blurred visions confuse
Her perching face, her thirst and warmth
Knowing all the way it is
The same as one who long since ceased.

72. Re-introspection

An anguish
Creeping as
Time eludes me

A feeling
Snailing at worthless moments
Spent in hurry

A feeling of torment
Crawling into words of selfishness
Uttered at You

A feeling that swallows,
Leaves Me disturbed
is a feeling of angst
that creeps, snails and crawls
As thoughts, movements, words.

73. Inquest

You could have said, "I'm all yours"
Before you quaked and turned in thunderous bliss.
Now,
I exhume your passion night by night
And bathe it in forensic yellow light
And scan the copper-smooth skin with my verse
For clues: my love must have an imprint left.

74. The Summer Garden

I watered them in the evening
Raising their summer scorched hues
To smile faintly and thank me for the showers
With love and care
Some bent towards me in blessing
Flowers heaving and sighing in the cold rolling down
Never to reach the parched below
Earth sucking in the puddles
Sending out an earthy perfume of happiness
Of asters, flocks and bluebells swaying in the wind
Now hidden in the green now in the open
Playing with the wind
Leaves sticking to petals as feathers to water
Clinging to the green for a life soon no more
The dried leaves on to the ground in droplets

Amidst the hues rise myriad wings
Like crystal sparkles
Playing with flowers happy
Hopping and dancing from one to another
Bees butterflies and insects numerous
Drinking the calm and peace
Quenching themselves in drops of honey and shower
Gossiping hitherthither

Falling from the heavy drops
Caught in a flower or blown by the wind
Getting ready to end the day
After a burnt scorching summer smell.

75. The Sun-the Eye-the Word

For the other,
This impatient wait
At the threshold
Of eluding words.
Wrestling and wresting
Thoughts,
Letters, words,
Sentences,
Gently amidst the skein
The svelte finger
Nimbly flutters.
The indifferent white
Waits to be stained
With words kneaded,
Together beaded,
Made poesie,
For you.

76. Spectrum

And I asked myself
Why this writing profuse!
The words replied:
We like spring
Fill your pages with colours
Moving out of you into the open
we merge
in others
to form a
rainbow:
A rainbow of your life

77. Ebb

A life pent up with broken hopes
About to burst from its heart and
Turn to smithereens:
The pain of your hope,
The burden of your life,
Welling clear at the shores
Of your eyes,
A feeble river
Rolling down, then dripping
To be sucked
By a parched surface;
To be lost in the arid vast;
The pain and its splintered hopes.
A heaviness
Remains
Moistening your being
Trying to wipe away
You and everything black:
Receding,
Ignored and alone.

78. A Blurb for the Age of Books

Rustling
Resting
Dusty and Yellow
Speeches in black
Of a culture born and bred
Of lives lived and lost

79. *Shards*

Poems that came
and existed of us
came to an end
the other day
as I came to know
it meant else to you.

You and I

It became mine again
as before
though I heard echoes –
splinters were crashing
somewhere far,
and one, in glassy flight,
scraped a neverhealed wound.

80. The Trip Back

Goddess, the wounds from your dagger-words haven't
quite healed.
Like a batch of seasoned butchers, they had flayed my
days quite skillfully;
I have come to hate the cuticles that newly sprouted
Under your studied tender nursing.

I have a nostalgia for the seething unskinned day
Now, in this meek new recuperance you've graced me
with.

In the mopped tidy room, on the table, white papers
and an ink-drunk pen;
a scrupled shelf, a sparse chair and a wooden cot;
a memory-snuffed ashtray; four whitewash-smelling
undecorated walls.

Like it was before you.

81. Cloud burst

Swollen eyes
Twitching cheeks
Hardly containing
Pain
Hurt
Sadness
Heaviness –

And a stream of tears

82. I'm Tired of You

I'm tired of you:
Bearing the weight
Of your lies lifeless
Like a cloak Diomede.

I'm tired of you:
Shed yourself.
Strip naked and
Be true to Life.

I'm tired of you:
Put me to bed.
Close my eyes to
Darkness.

83. Twirl

Every day rehearses
The Eternal Whiteness of the Last Day
When out of Time's bright womb
Cuddled Twins shall be born.

Every night rehearses
The Eternal Dark of the Last Night
Where the foci of all things fuse:
Streets smoothing the edifices
Become fields once again;
Wheels shedding friction
Become feet once again.

From their fire shall you know them
For their leaving leaves no traces of the Day;
From their music shall you know them
For their cadence tides the blood of Night.

Every lived moment resurges
The events of the First Day
When out of a Cuddled Twins
The very Time was born.

84. She Likes Us to Walk
the Busy City-Roads

Anonymity is a function of these roads:
It is festival week
And the noisy city night
Rubbed our pasts off our names.

Among the clamor of the bazaar
I see your face receiving
The evening's chimerical patterns,
As moving lights kiss and flee the moving us;

I turn my eyes up
To study the patterns
Of April stars
As you stop at a bangle shop
To bargain in vain.

The stars seemed like
Broken lights from an exhibit-design
That tried to replicate the bazaar ground.

They held the moon in a hazy wet bowl of light
and whispered through a hustle of the wind
How anonymity is their idea of a night.

85. Tentacles

The mortal Gorgon sister
Hissing Meduse tentacles
Assurgent live ail –
Aloft mounting rising
And gliding
Ascendente
Wincing windblown tresses
Wind down
Halter

86. His Webbiness

I threw myself down from my stately twig -
The world rose to me, I said: 'Enough! Halt!'
And bounced royally on a line velvet
I spun (and checked again the safety tug).

I spin around in golden morning air
My legs drawn, like a swollen furry seed,
And burst suddenly - ah, a star's affair! -
To weave a diaphanous webby deed.

Each thread conveys a lustrous call to play
A token game of death in malice groomed -
I move the same, piteous prey astray,
Remember, habitually well-assumed.

87. The After-rain Eve

Water streaming
Thunder rumbling
Damp pleasant shadows
Soaking dripping foliages
Wind chill, shrilling
Bubbles meeting their destiny
Before destination is reached
A cold wind piercing the face
As I walk
An after-rain Eve
The icy cool aching in me:
In the warmth of my clothes
A cold neck and face
A frozen hand and feet
Feeling the drops coldly disappearing
As the wind blows on my dress
And glues it to me.

88. Describing

I'm trying to describe how I feel
When you take leave of me
At the end of the day
And I see a brown bird breaking
Out of lone clouds
With full throated calls
Wings majestically still
And my hands like ants' tentacles
Searching to comprehend the largeness
Of a strange thing that fills the void
Move up the air in front.

And I'm trying to describe how I feel
When you take leave of me
At the end of the day.

89. Onward

Life lived
By each step
Up
Down
Up and Down
Keeping me on my toes
As sweat drenched I
Whizz past the roads
Caught in traffic blocks
And serpentine queues
Where people push and nudge
To get past
Moving from one to the other

90. She Saunters into the Sun

She saunters into the sun
And then into the shade
Up the wall now and
Now onto a dreamy world
Purring, clutching, hiding behind darkly leaves,
pillars or trees
To pounce on the shivering inexistent.

Now in heaviness majestically spreading
Her feline self
She studies, licks her own soft purr
Cuddles inside herself.
A gymnast,
Her paws one before the other
Move into glistening clutches and clawings
Leaving behind screeches guttural.

Ears alert, eyes scansorial
Her nose twitches sharp
And leads her leaps and jaunts
Into a beckoning wild world.

91. To be an Artist among Other Things

As the artist carried
The crying child outside the house
And showed him the starry sky,
He noted that
Each suspended tear
In the baby's eyes
Made a hanging moon.

92. Raindrops

rain d
      r
        o
         p
          s

wet   cold
and   s
           l
             a
               n
                 t

Into   Life
pouring
showers from above

93. Time

Time   sleep
          ticks   in a blissful
                and   ends
                    Life

94. Waves

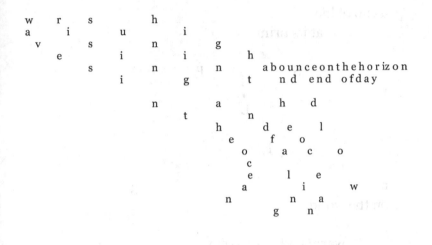

95. Elixir and the Cup

a cup of life
        at its brim

             S   P
I
                    L

              l
   i
n   g
on the world

    warm and cozy to sip

       steaming cup SCALDING

96.

m

       a

     r

     b

     l

e

      s

     r

     o

     l

     l

     i

     n

     g

     d

     o

     w

     n

h   e

     l

  t

       e   r   s k   el   ter

d ow n the i

        n

         c

          l

           i

            n

       lost   for   e v e r in the r u n

97. It's Raining Us

...ifeltthedrops

      falling

         n

gliding ...

        down..

myface..

      anoceanof

        salt....

PUSHING

fromwithin.....

ofdrops

bl

      own

inthewind

        fromYOU

     to

        ME

and

to

        US

98. A Day Folded in Stars

Higher and Higher
Above
And then into
The clouds
Tearing them, piercing
The white foam.
A rumbling ocean.

In the sky of
Grey calm
Dull and dim
Cupping a fiery orange
A line of scarlet.

Then night and dark.
Sweeping down
Into the darkness,
Flickering multitudes:
A starry earth.

99. The Night Bus

A street winked.
Darkness.
The fading smear of a wall.
A darting bridge.
A lonely dog.
Hurrying asphalt.
A company of smokers.

It is hard to come to terms with:
the world only absently watches
as I, windowed, nightwards vanish.

100. Soul Lake

This night, dear, holds the lake of your soul
Where lotus leaves bob in blue winds;
Its sacred nakedness is
A mirror to hold ripe stars falling from the abysses of
the sky.
I dip in, disintegrate and splash up
As pinkly blossoms all over your surface
And gasp at the sky, every time, in pleasure.

Printed in the United States
by Baker & Taylor Publisher Services

Printed in the United States
By Bookmasters